BEDTIME HUGS
for LITTLE ONES

About the Author and the Artist

This is the first children's book by recording artist and actress Debby Boone, illustrated by her husband, Gabriel Ferrer. Featured in the book are their four children – son Jordan, twin girls Gabrielle and Dustin, and the youngest, Tessa. The family pet, Tex the Mouse, also puts in a special appearance. Debby, Gabriel, and their family live in southern California.

BEDTIME HUGS *for* LITTLE ONES

Copyright © 1988 by Resi, Inc.
Published by Harvest House Publishers
Eugene, Oregon 97402
www.harvesthousepublishers.com

Library of Congress Cataloging-in-Publication Data

Boone, Debby.
     Bedtime Hugs for little ones.

     Summary: A collection of short pieces for bedtime, including "Counting Sheep," "Prayer Time," and "Beds and Spaceships."
     1. Children's stories, American.   [1. Bedtime–Fiction. 2. Short stories]
I. Ferrer, Gabriel, ill.   II. Title.   III. Title: Bedtime hugs for little ones.
PZ7.B64593Be   1988   [E]   87-81035
ISBN 0-89081-616-6 (hardcover)
ISBN 0-7369-1378-5 (paperback)

Design and production by Koechel Peterson and Associates, Inc.,
Minneapolis, Minnesota

Printed in China

04 05 06 07 08 / IM / 5 4 3 2 1

BEDTIME HUGS
for LITTLE ONES

Debby Boone

Illustrated by Gabriel Ferrer

HARVEST HOUSE PUBLISHERS

EUGENE, OREGON

A NICE TIME

You can say I love you
almost any time.

You can say it when you're very happy
and want someone to share your smile.

You can say it when you're very sad
and just need a hug.

You can say it for no reason at all
just because you thought of it.

But there's something nice,
very nice...

About saying it
when you're all tucked in
and the covers are just cozy
and the pillow is just where you want it.

Then you reach up
and whisper it
so that just one other person
in the whole wide world
can hear you.

Night time is a nice time
to say I love you.

BATH TIME

Did you have a bath tonight?

Did you splash the water till it looked like rain?
Did you make a wave with your arm to sink a paper ship?
Did you have so many bubbles that you couldn't see your own toes?
Did you make a beard or a hat with the bubbles?
Did you blow them in the air
until it looked like snowflakes
falling back down into the tub?
Did you lose the soap
and finally find it under the washcloth,
where it had been hiding all the time?
Did you see how funny your hair looked
when it's wet and sticking to your head?

I think the nicest thing about a bath
is that everything from that whole day—
fingerpaint,
dirt from playing in the backyard,
noodles from dinner,
ice cream smudges from dessert—
everything
washes away ...
and you're ready to start tomorrow
clean and fresh.

I think *that's* why you feel so warm and nice
when you get out! ❤

COUNTING SHEEP

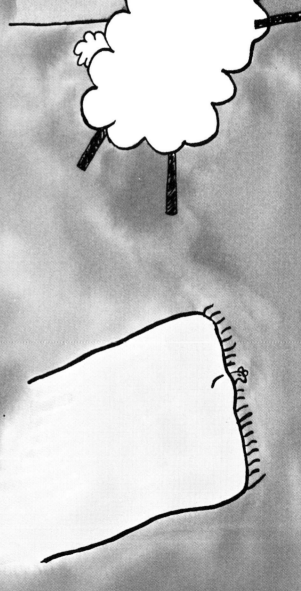

Someone a long time ago
(I don't know who or when)
once said, "If you have trouble sleeping,
try counting sheep."
Then they said to close your eyes
(no fair peeking)
and imagine fluffy white sheep
jumping over a white picket fence.

That's never worked for me.
I close my eyes...I start counting...
but I have a problem.
My sheep start getting silly.
They dance, they sing, they carry on,
and generally make it *impossible* for me to sleep.

Another person once said, "Don't count sheep.
Fall asleep counting your blessings."
I like that.
Let's try it.
Close your eyes.
Now think of all the things you have been given...
Your family. Your favorite toys.
Birds and trees and blue skies.
Pretty soon you start smiling...
and you close your eyes...
and all of a sudden—
you're asleep. ❤

BLANKETS

Do you have a favorite blanket?
One with the alphabet on it
or one where bunnies hop around?

Blankets have a way of making you feel
safe,
like you're being hugged all the time.
And you can feel it
the minute you first start getting into bed.

You pull your blankets back
into a triangle,
and then you slip your legs into them
and then slide all the way down.

I like blankets
when they're not under your shoulder
(where they could slip down)
and not over your nose
(where it could get too stuffy)
but just under your chin,
tucked all around you.

That's when I think blankets are the
best. ❤

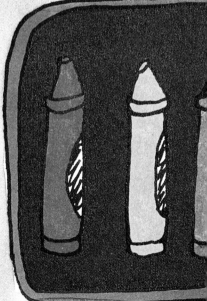

SHOOTING STARS

Most stars don't move.

You look up in the sky,
and the same star you saw last night
will also be up there tonight
and tomorrow night
and the night after that
and most likely next year, too.

Shooting stars, on the other hand, like to move.
They like to move fast—
faster than you or I ever could.

Some people say
that they move so fast
they burn up.

Others say
that it's just God's way
of wishing the world
a good night's sleep...

Kind of like blowing a big kiss. ♥

RAIN AT NIGHT

Drip, drop.
Drip, drop.
Listen, can you hear it?
Wait—there it is again.
Drip, plip. Clatter, clatter, clatter.
The rain has started.

I like rain at night.
It's fun knowing that it's splashy wet outside—
wet houses, wet roofs, wet windows.
But inside it's dry and warm.
And you can just listen—
to drops on wet pavement,
to tires as they wash around curbs.

Remember the first time it rained?
Noah? The Flood?
Animals staying warm and dry inside the ark
while water swirled around outside?
Remember what Noah saw
when it finished raining?

Remember? The rainbow.
That was God's way of promising
that the rain would always stop.
And God *always* keeps His promises.

Maybe we'll see a rainbow tomorrow. ♥

GROWING

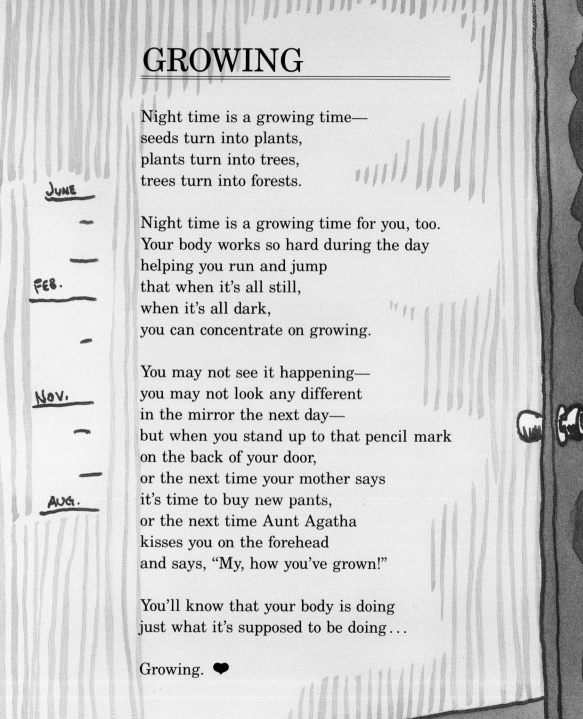

JUNE

FEB.

NOV.

AUG.

Night time is a growing time—
seeds turn into plants,
plants turn into trees,
trees turn into forests.

Night time is a growing time for you, too.
Your body works so hard during the day
helping you run and jump
that when it's all still,
when it's all dark,
you can concentrate on growing.

You may not see it happening—
you may not look any different
in the mirror the next day—
but when you stand up to that pencil mark
on the back of your door,
or the next time your mother says
it's time to buy new pants,
or the next time Aunt Agatha
kisses you on the forehead
and says, "My, how you've grown!"

You'll know that your body is doing
just what it's supposed to be doing...

Growing. ❤

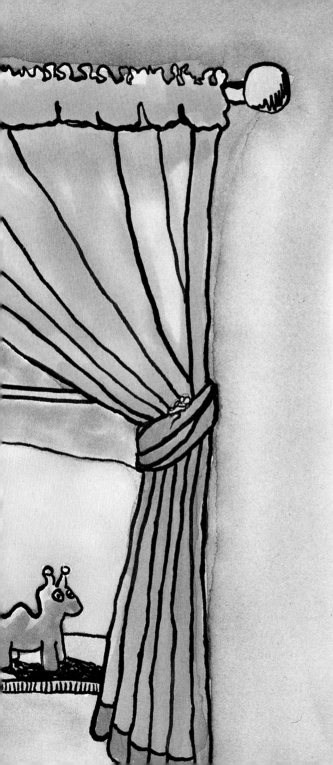

WHERE
THE SUN GOES

Where does the sun go at night?
Ever wonder?

The world is so big and round
that the sun just can't get to it
all at once.

So when you are getting ready for bed,
the sun is going to another part of the world,
where someone just your age
is getting up
and eating breakfast
and getting ready for school.

The sun never stops shining.
You just can't always see it,
but it's always there.

And you know one thing for sure—
Just as your name is...
well, whatever your name is,
the sun will be back
tomorrow
morning...

Right on time! ❤

TOMORROW

You know, that's a great word—
"tomorrow."

Tomorrow you're
one day closer to Christmas,
one day closer to your birthday,
one day closer to trying something new.

Forget yesterday.
If you haven't been able to hop on one foot,
maybe tomorrow.
If you haven't been able to reach the light
switch,
maybe tomorrow.
If you haven't been able to jump this far,
maybe tomorrow.

Tomorrow you could—
    Call someone you love
    Draw a picture
    Say something nice
    Try something new.

Tomorrow is a new day,
and it could be your *best* day.

What do you want to do tomorrow? ♥

PRAYER TIME

We say goodnight
to Daddy,
to Mama,
to the dog,
to the goldfish in the bowl sitting on the dresser,
to our favorite toys.

But remember how much God looks forward
to saying goodnight to us, too.
He loves to hear
what we enjoyed during the day,
what we need for tomorrow,
what we felt sad about,
what we felt bad about.

God loves you more than anyone else could,
and He looks forward to that time of night
when you can share your thoughts with Him.

And when you say "Amen"
and it's time to close your eyes
and when Mama and Daddy leave the room,
remember…

He's still there
all through the night,
watching over us. ♥

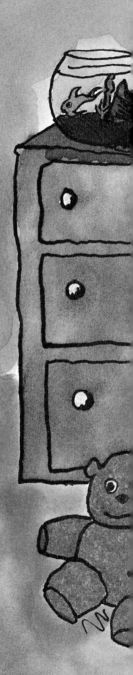

BEDS AND
SPACESHIPS

Let's turn your bed into a spaceship,
and you can make it go
wherever you want it to go.

How about
to a different part of the city—
to your grandmother's house,
where she could bake you cookies...

Or to a different part of the world—
to darkest Africa,
where you could sneak up on lions and tigers
and watch them with their baby cubs...

Or how about way out—
into outer space,
to the Milky Way,
where you could look back at an earth
the size of one of your grandmother's
cookies?

If your bed were a spaceship,
where would you go? ♥

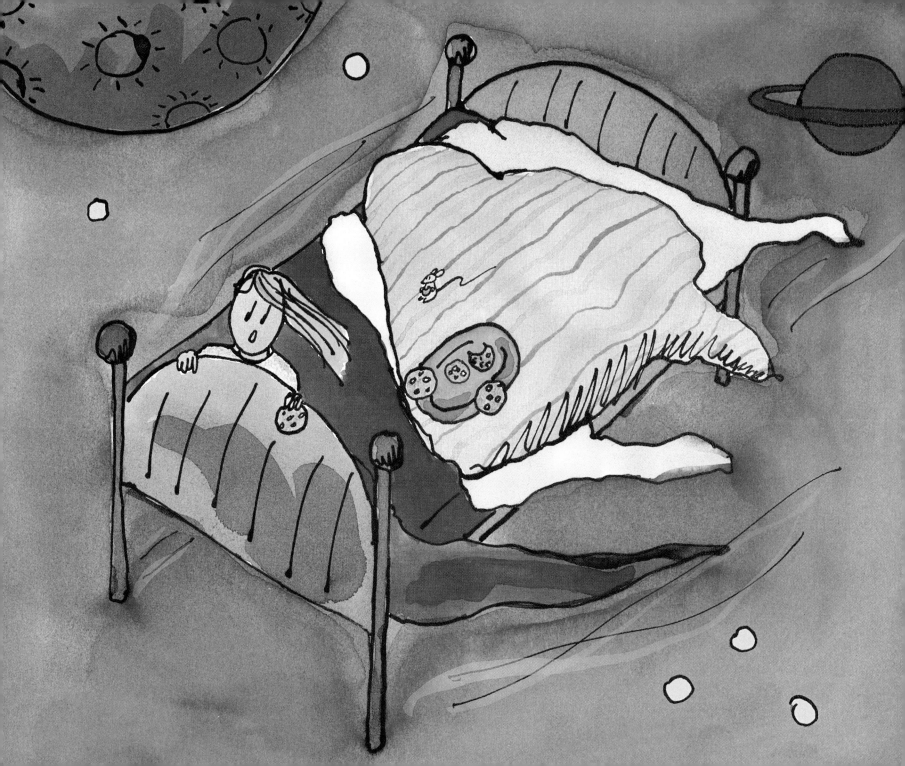

FUNNY DREAMS

Have you ever had a dream
that was *so* funny
that you woke up laughing?

I had a dream once
where I was real hungry,
so hungry I could have eaten my nose!

And then
all of a sudden
my nose started to grow
larger and larger
and longer and longer,
and then it turned green
and then it turned . . .
into a big dill pickle!

So I broke it off,
dipped it into a jar of mustard,
and ate it.

And then I woke up—
laughing. ♥

THE DARK

Dark dark places are no fun.
Dark dark rooms,
dark dark houses,
dark dark stairways—
they kinda give you the creeps.
You know...
the chills,
the willies,
the heebee-jeebies.
Dark dark places are no fun at all.

But you know what?
Sort of dark isn't that bad.
In fact, sort of dark is *good*.

Did you know that God made the dark?
That's right.
The first day God made
both day *and* night...
and He said it was *good*.

Good so that things could quiet down,
good to give our eyes a rest,
good to make it easy to go to sleep.

I guess that
sort of dark really is good. ♥

WHEN YOU GROW UP

When you grow up, what will you be?
You don't have to decide now,
but it's fun to think about.

Will you be—
A painter or a president?
An actor or an astronaut?
A doctor or a discoverer?

You don't have to just pick one, either.
You can pick two
or even three
if you want to.

When you grow up
you could think about different things all day
(they call that a philosopher)
or you could make speeches and quote other people
(they call that a politician)
or you could take care of a zoo
so you could see all your favorite animals every day.

And just because you wanted to be something yesterday
doesn't mean that you can't pick something different today.

I wonder what you'll be when you grow up? ♥

THE MOON

The moon has lots of faces.

He has a big round face—
maybe just a tiny bit orange
shining bright into the night
for all to see.
He looks very happy!

Sometimes he shows
just a sliver of a face,
like a fingernail tilted down.
He looks tired and sleepy.

When there is a ring around him
and he seems kind of far off
and is small and hazy,
he looks sad.

And when he's feeling
a little bit shy...

You won't see him at all. ❤

FAVORITE TOY

At our house we have a rule—
you can take *one* toy to bed.

It's a hard choice to make.
You don't want something that's too hard
(like a truck or a train),
you don't want something with too many pieces
(like a puzzle),
you don't want something messy
(like crayons),
you don't want something that makes a lot of
noise
(like a toy piano),
and it's never a good idea to pick the doll
that wants to play and jump on your bed
and get you into trouble.

You want to choose a *good* toy.

Try the stuffed bunny missing one ear
over in the corner
that looks like he doesn't want to be alone.

Maybe he could be your favorite toy tonight. ❤

GOOD NIGHT SOUNDS

If you close your eyes
and keep very still,
you might hear...

The soft music of a radio,
a neighbor's dog barking a long way off,
cars quietly whooshing by,
a plane high overhead
   taking tired people to their homes.

In the summer...a cricket chirp.
In the winter...the hum of a heater.
In the spring and fall...the low whisper of wind.

These are the good night sounds,
and all of them
are softly saying to you,
Good night! Sleep sweet! Good night! ♥

JUST AS YOU ARE

Promise me something.
Promise me
that you will always
remember one thing…

You are loved
and always will be,
not because you've done something special
  (although it's nice when you do),
and not because you haven't done anything wrong
  (although it's swell when you don't).

You are loved
because you are you,
and that can never change
and that *will* never change.

You are loved
just as you are
right this very moment. ♥